THIS NOTEBOOK BELONGS TO:

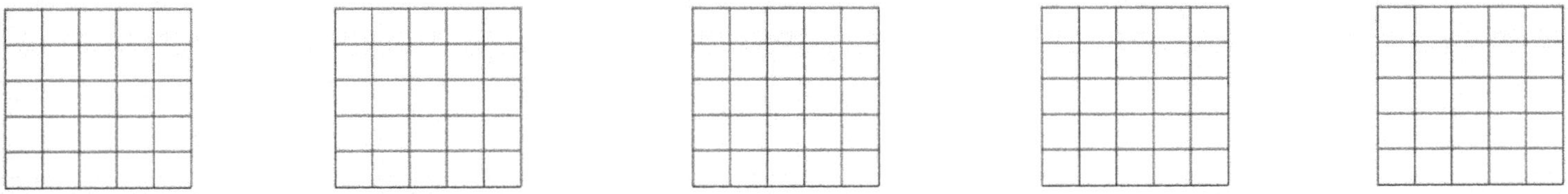

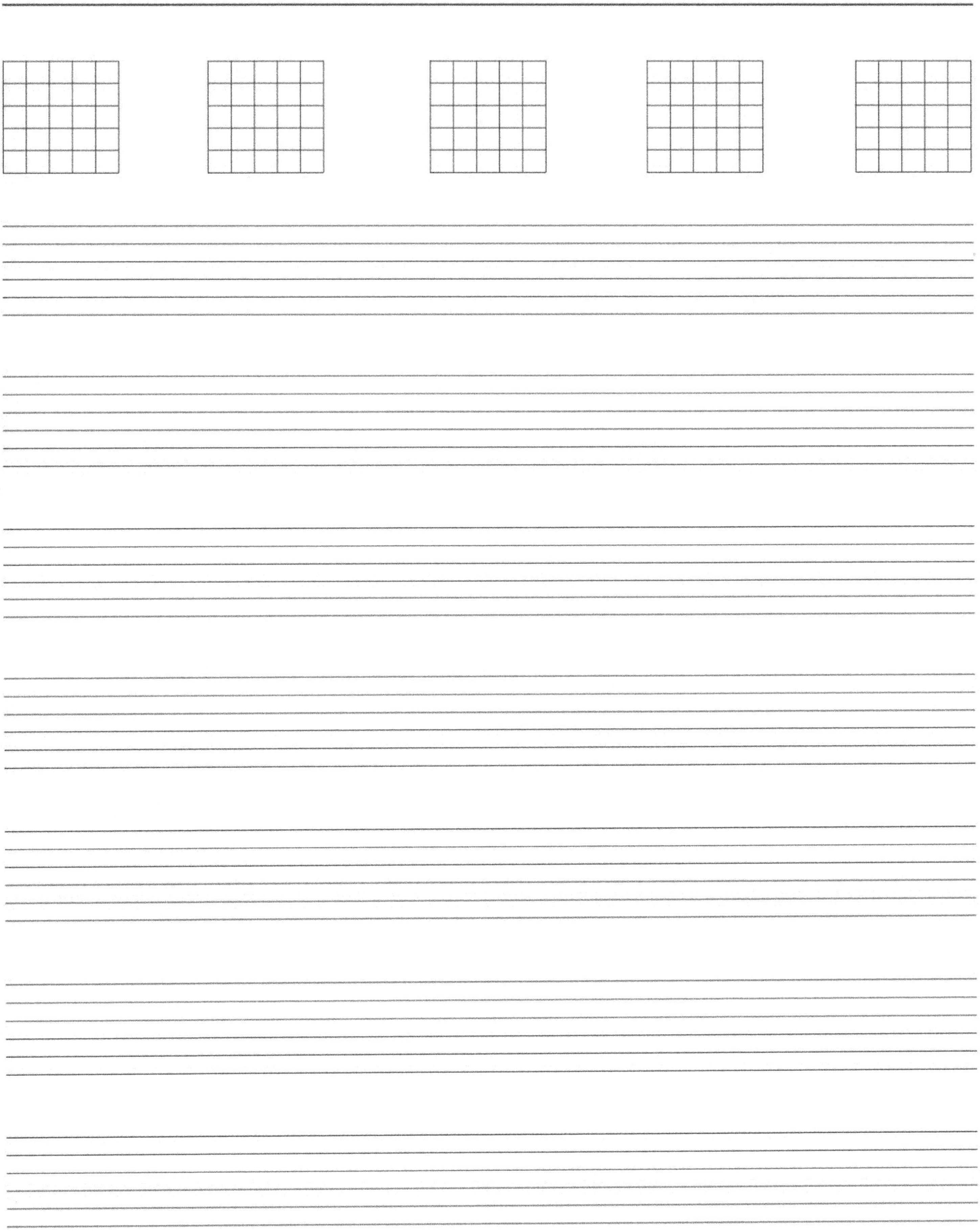

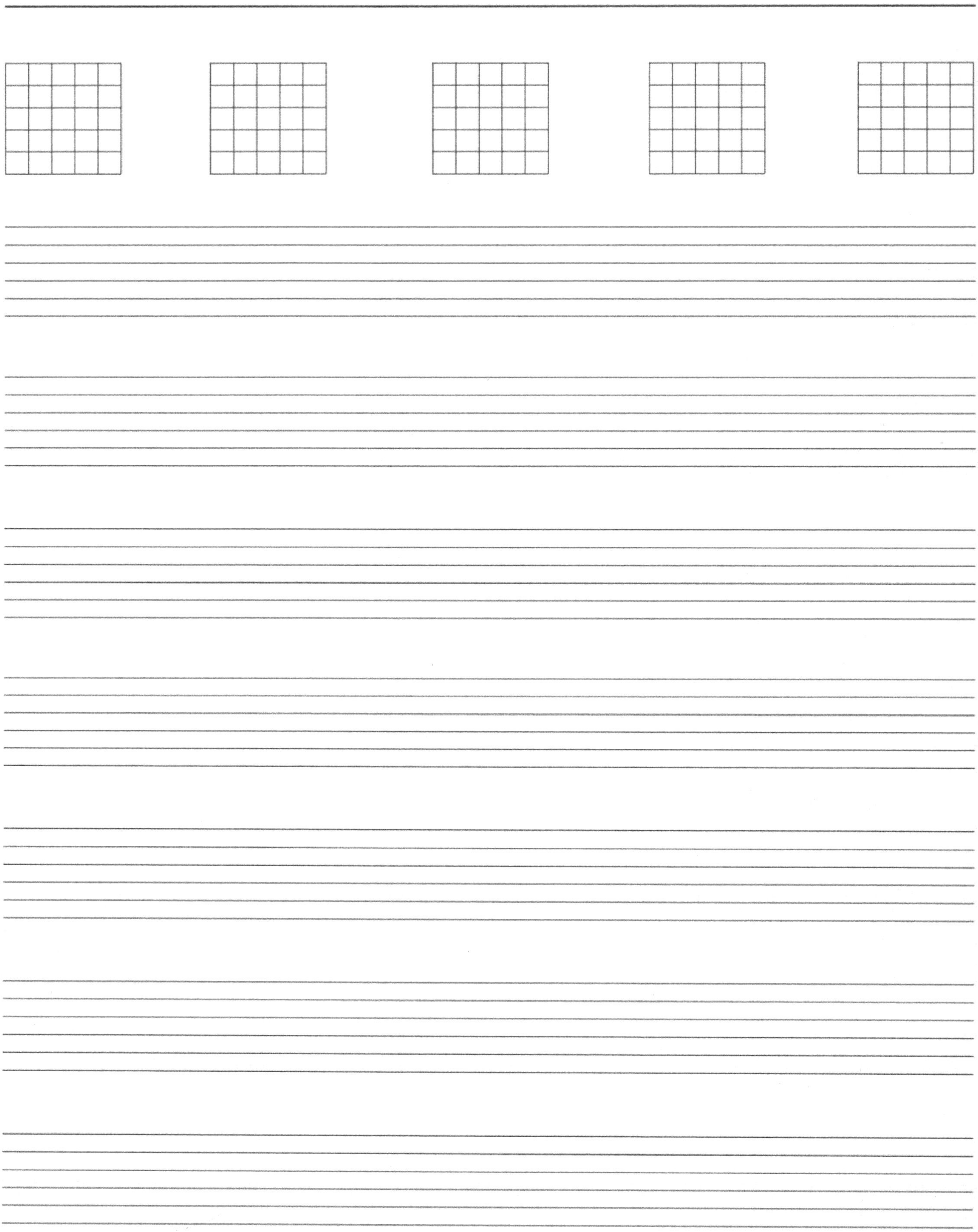

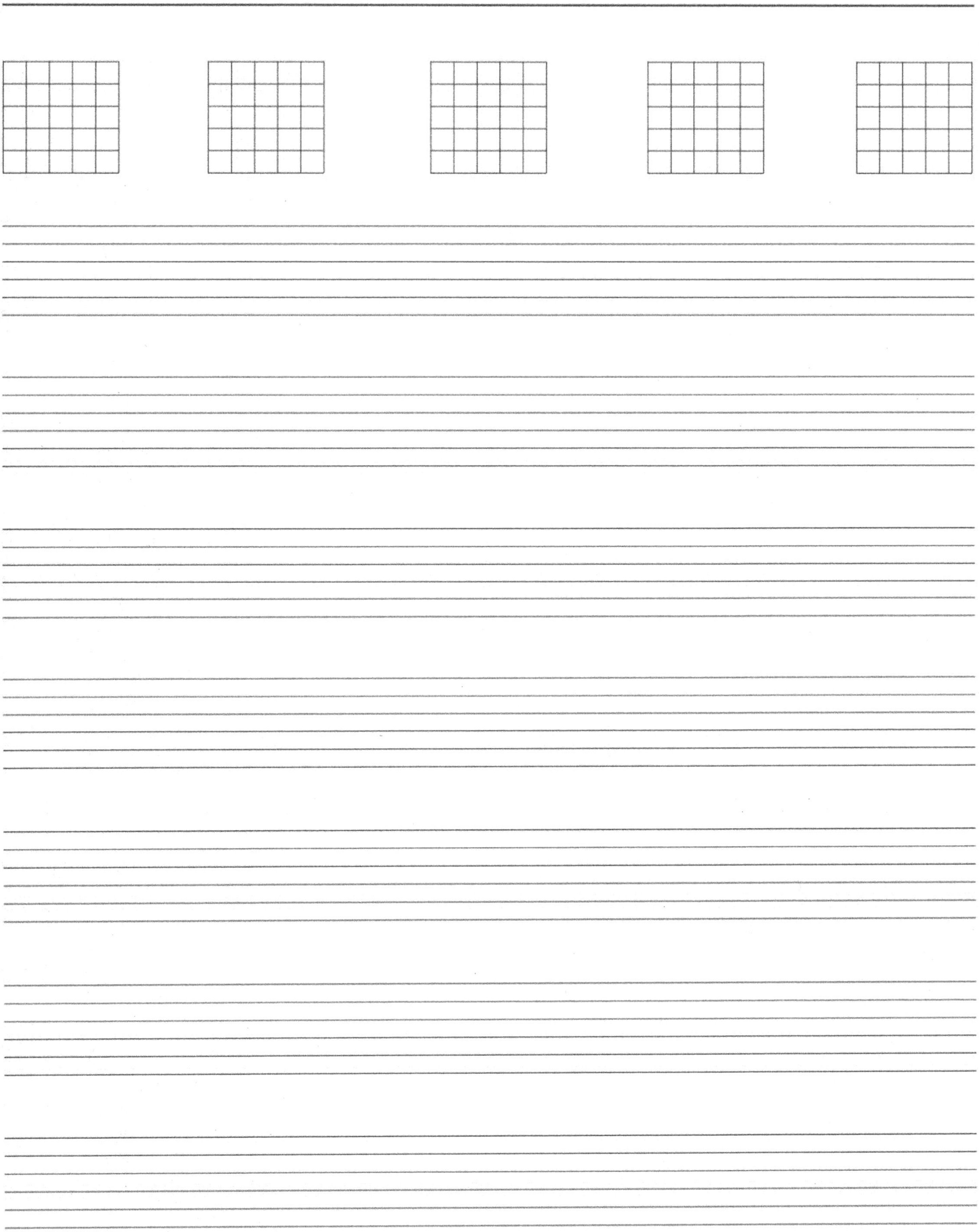

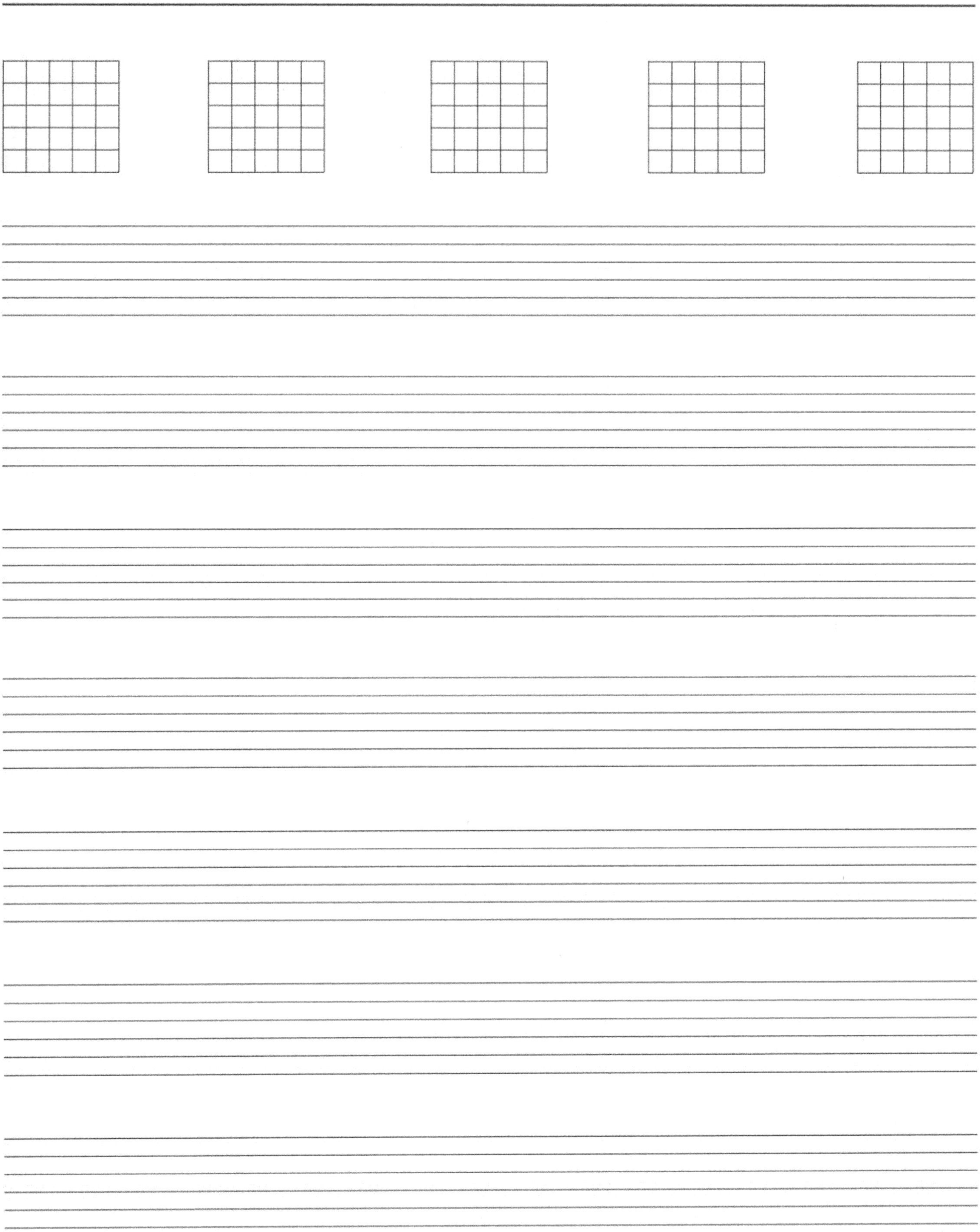

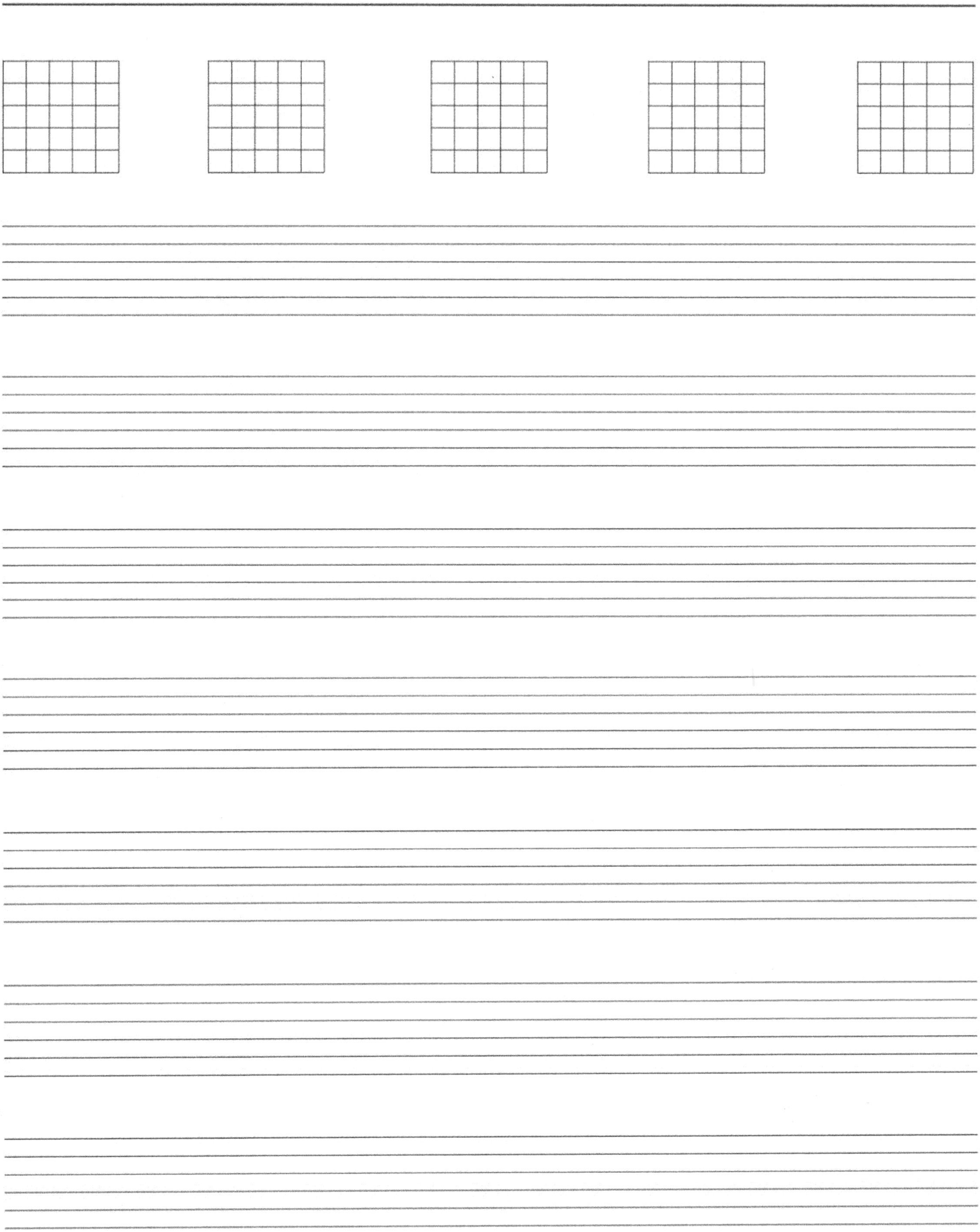

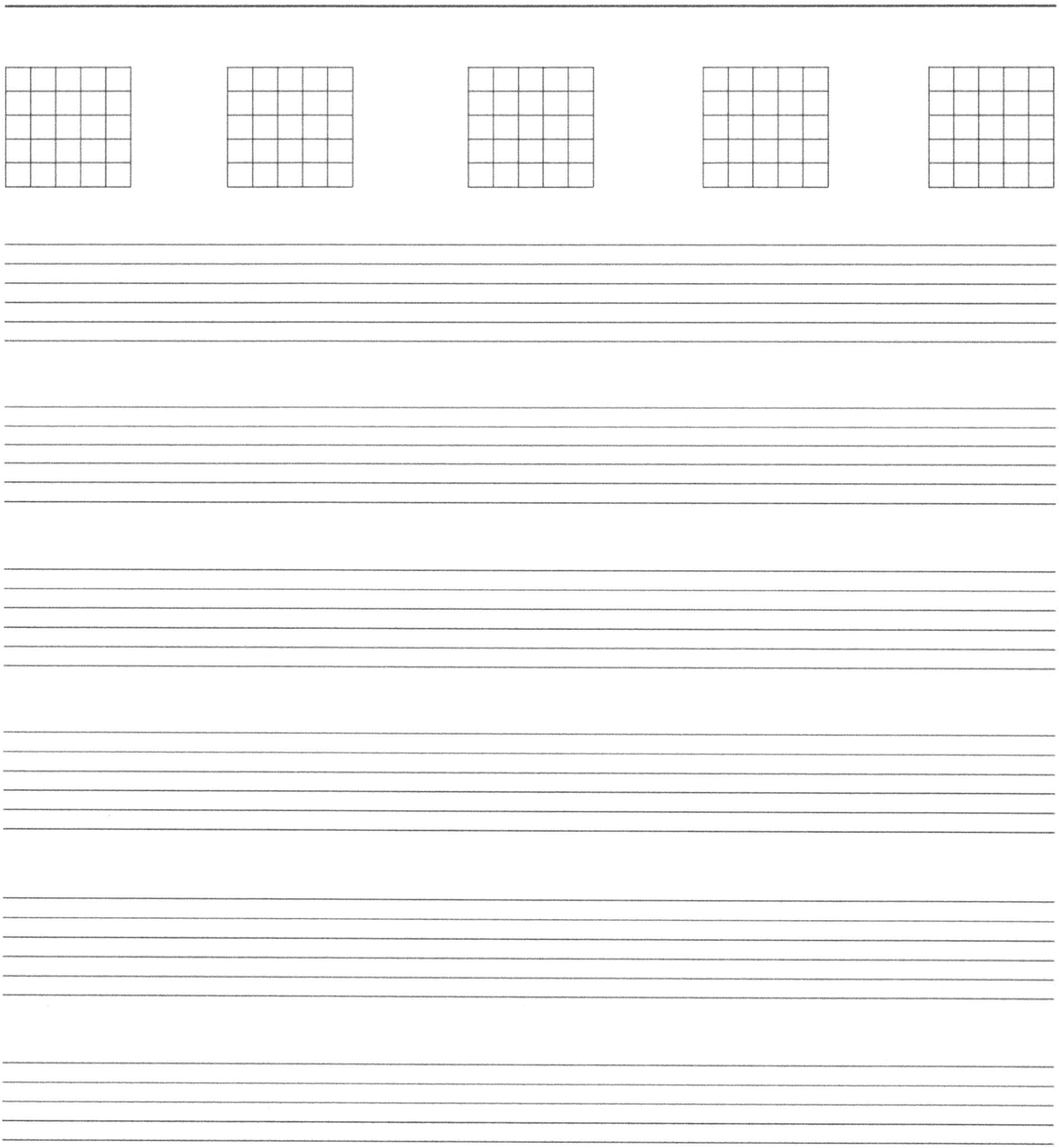

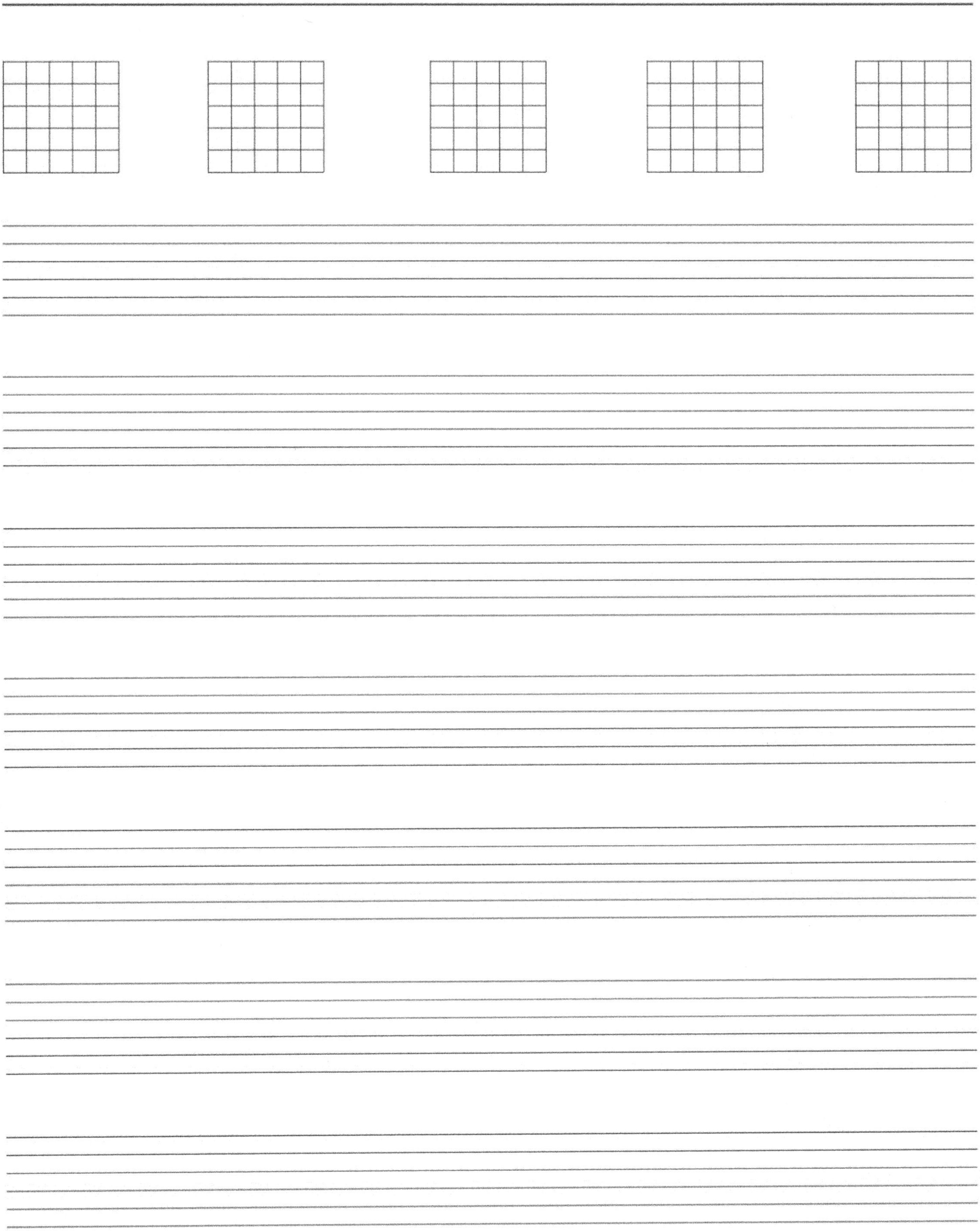

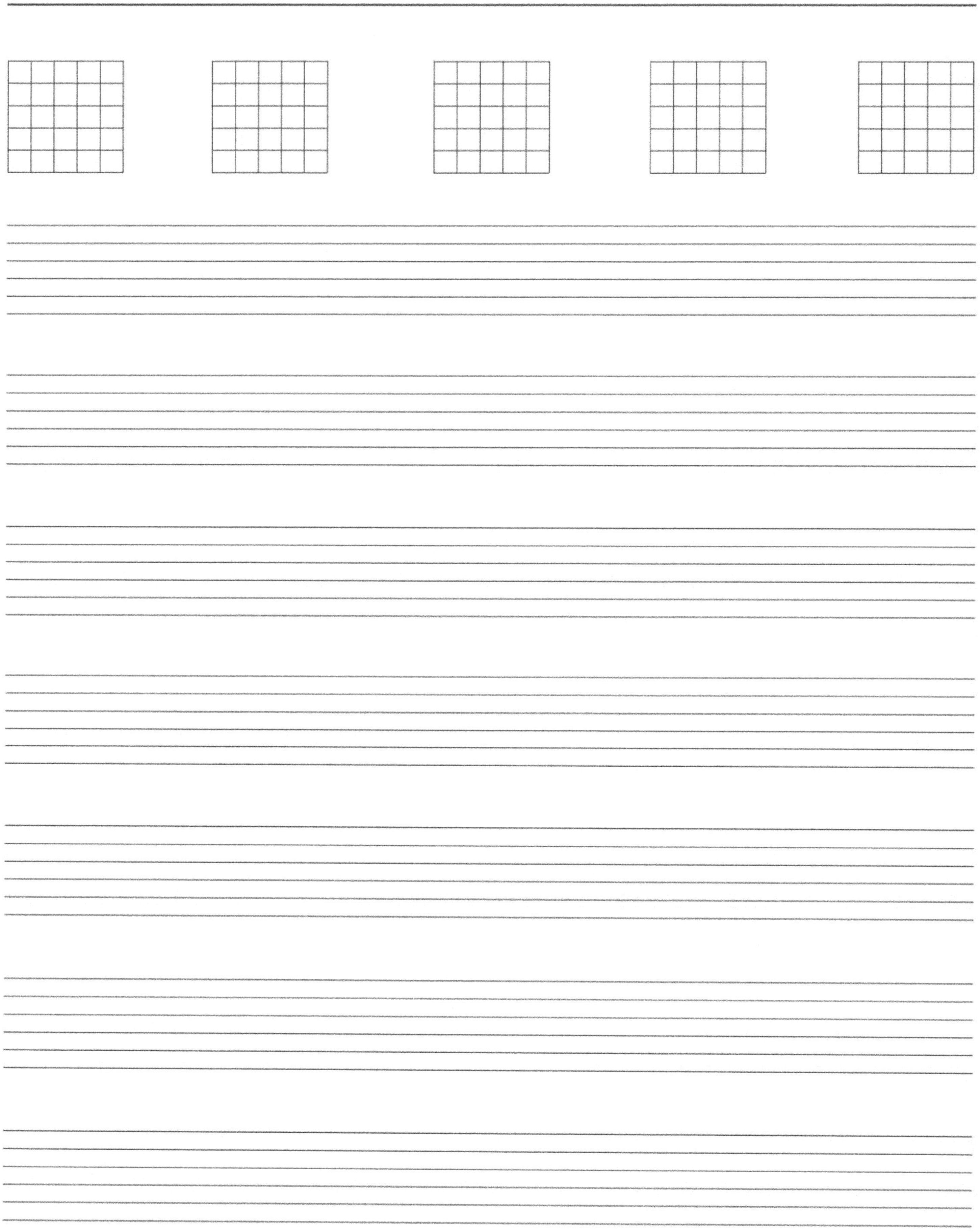

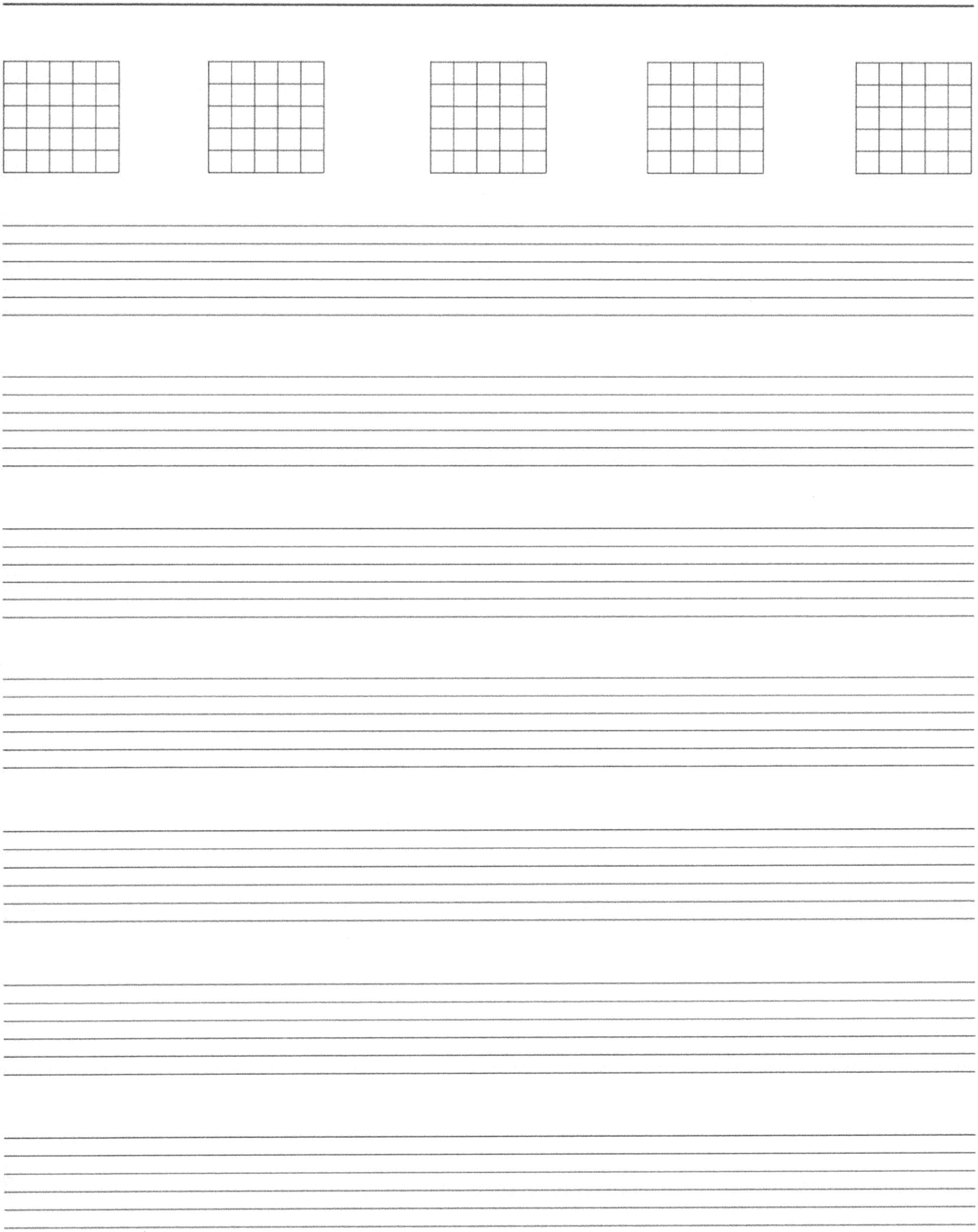

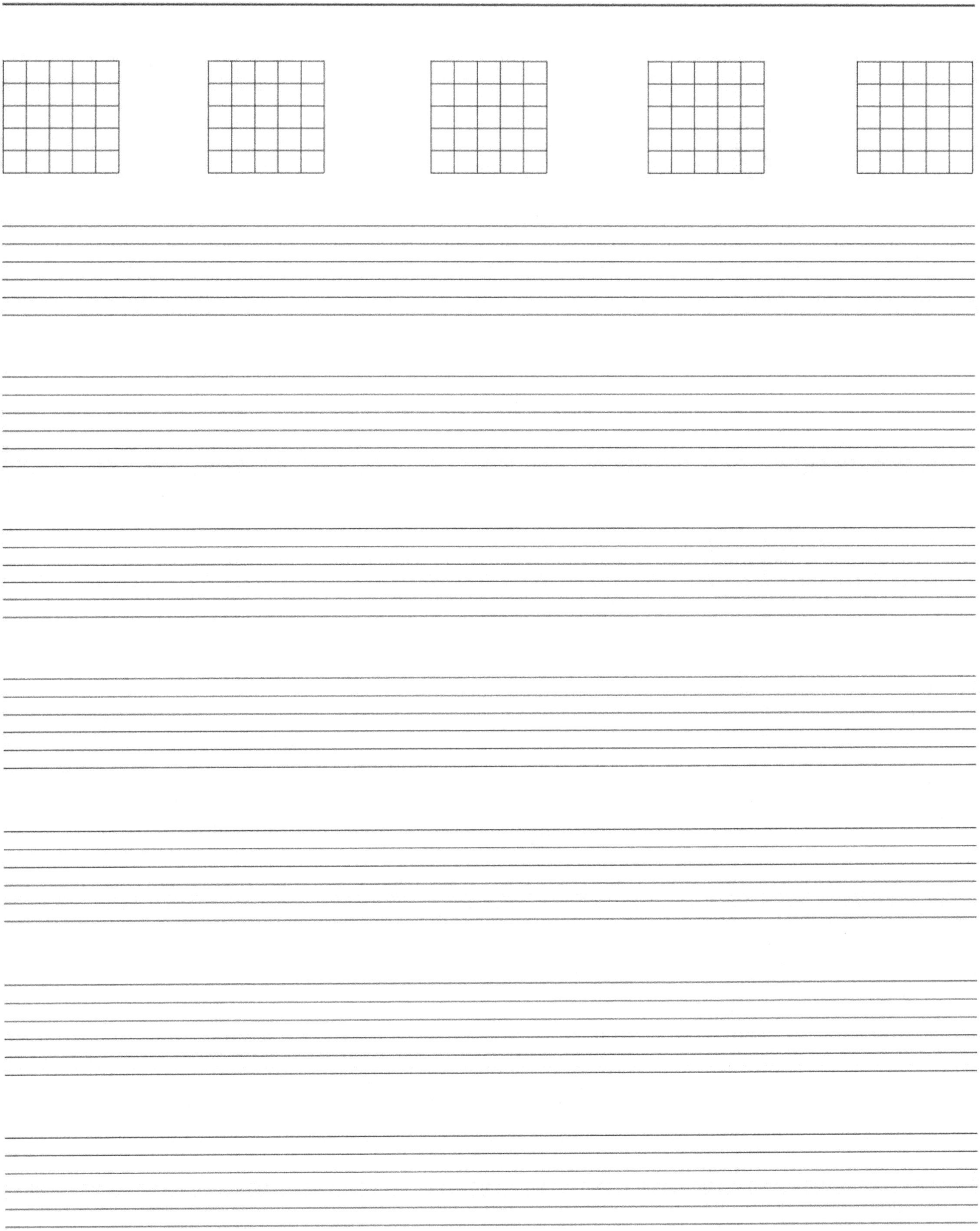

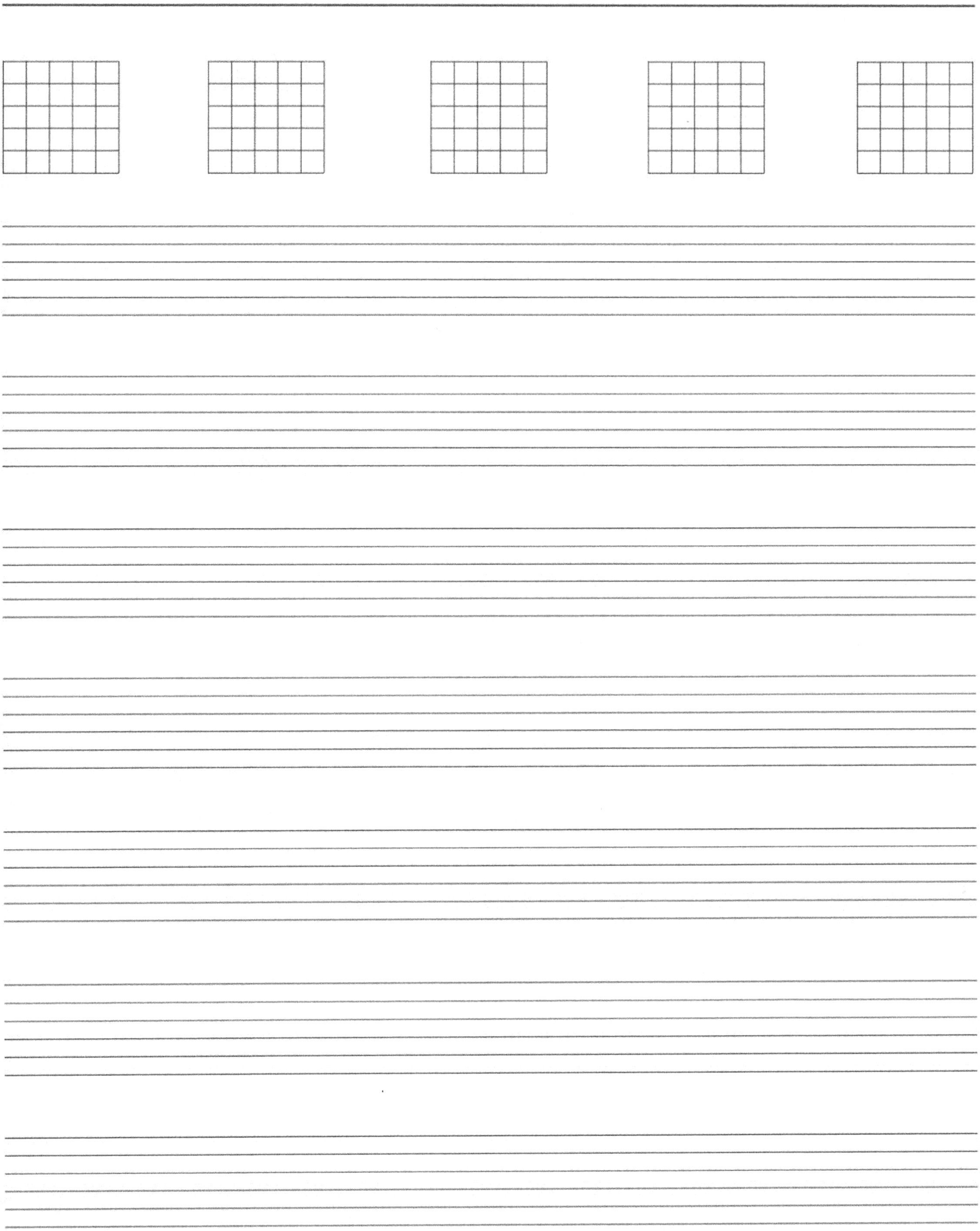

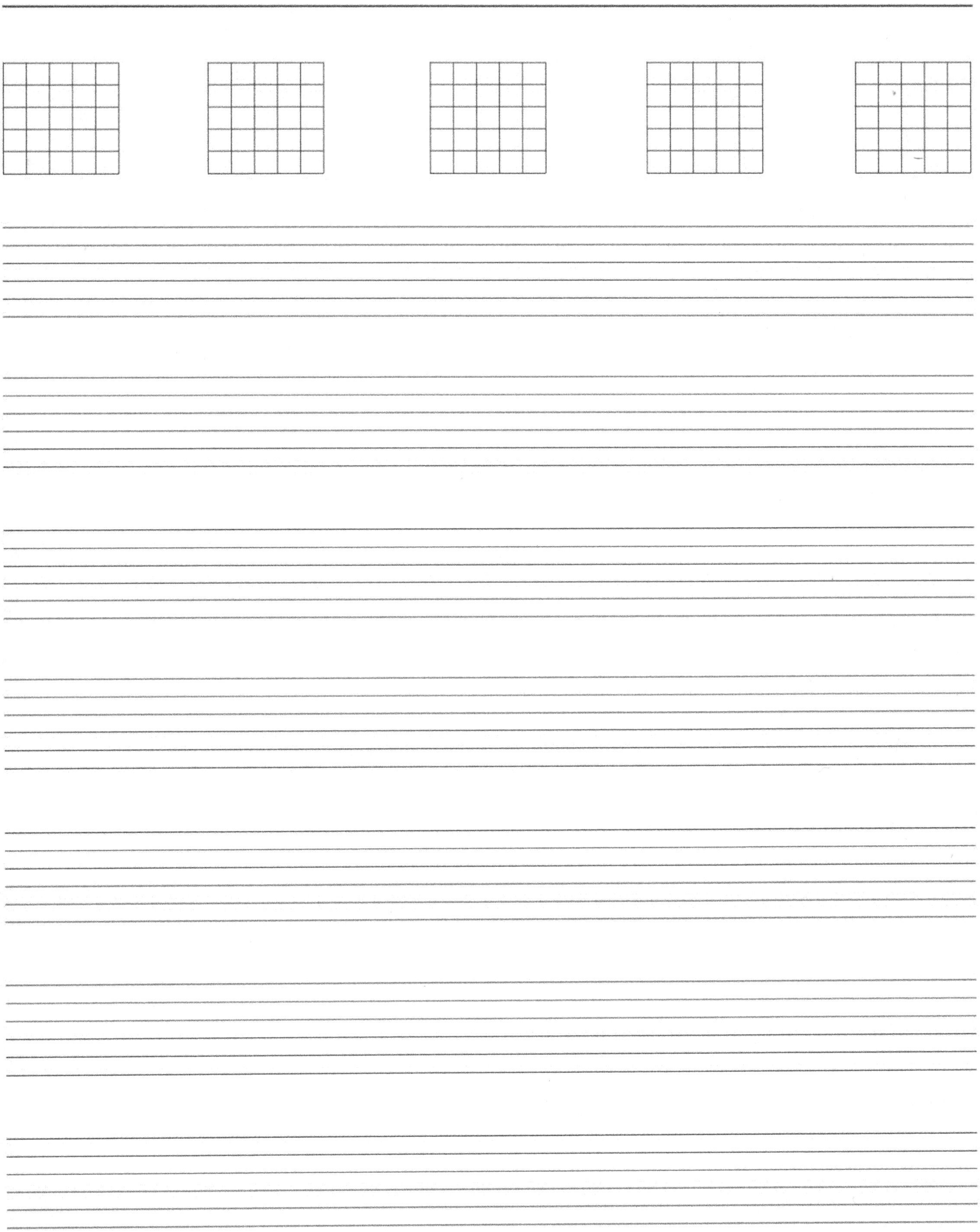

www.ingramcontent.com/pod-product-compliance
Lightning Source LLC
Chambersburg PA
CBHW080812210225
22282CB00057B/732
9785963668641